JETLINERS

Clinton H. Groves

Motorbooks International
Publishers & Wholesalers ®

Dedication

This book is dedicated to the memory of my mother, Irene Kelly Groves. Born Irene Kelly in Philadelphia in 1916, she was the daughter of an L&N Railroad Foreman. Growing up in Irvine, Ravenna, and Hazard, Kentucky, she became hooked on aviation the first time she saw a wood and fabric Waco biplane. Her dreams were shattered when upon graduating from Hazard High School her father, J. Kirklin Kelly, would not let her study Aeronautical Engineering. "Young ladies do not do that sort of thing" he told her. "You can take teaching or nursing; otherwise you stay at home."

I hope that I was able to make a difference in her life. We shared together many light-plane flights, and she was able to travel most of the globe through my twenty-three years' employment with TWA. She was more than a mother, she was a best friend.

First published in 1993 by Motorbooks International Publishers & Wholesalers, PO Box 2, 729 Prospect Avenue, Osceola, WI 54020 USA

Motorbooks International is a certified trademark, registered with the United States Patent Office

Motorbooks International books are also available at discounts in bulk quantity for industrial or sales-promotional use. For details write to Special Sales Manager at the Publisher's address

Printed and bound in Hong Kong

Library of Congress Cataloging-in-Publication Data
Groves, Clinton.
    Jetliners / Clinton Groves.
       p. cm. — (Enthusiast color series)
    Includes index.
    ISBN 0-87938-821-8
    1. Jet transports—History. I. Title. II.
Series.
TL685.7.G77   1993
629.133'349—dc20   93-13069

On the front cover: American 747-SP31, a former TWA jet, takes off from Dallas-Fort Worth, bound for Tokyo, on 25 August 1989. *Steve Tobey*

On the frontispiece: An Alaska Airlines 737-400 takes off from John Wayne Airport in Orange County, California. *Brian Gore*

On the title page: On 18 September 1979, the first McDonnell Douglas MD80 took to the air from Long Beach Airport in California. The first version, the MD81, is powered by two Pratt & Whitney JT8D-209 engines. Its fuselage length is 147 feet, 10 inches; wing span is 107 feet, 11 inches. In flight-testing one airplane destined for Swissair suffered such a hard landing that the tail broke off the airplane at the pressure bulkhead. One crew member was startled to open the rear door to the ventral stairs and find nothing there. The photo shows a TWA MD82 landing over snow on a bright, sunny day. *Dave Campbell*

On the back cover: A Braniff DC8 with the art work of Alexander Calder in 1973. *Nigel Chalcraft*

Contents

Acknowledgments

Things are always changing in the world of air transportation. Flying, but with no photo available, is the McDonnell Douglas MD90, a stretched MD80 with IAE V2500 engine. Also flying at this time is the Airbus Industrie A330.

There are also factoids—undocumented data or opinions not verified—in many publications of this sort. I have tried to keep all data as accurate as possible in the time allowed for research. Updates and corrections are always welcomed.

Special thanks go to Michael A. Sparkman of Huntsville, Alabama, for a lot of data research on very short notice. I prepared the color slides, color correcting and cropping each one until they were right while Mike spent most of his February 1993 vacation at the library. Without Mike's help, the short deadline would have been impossible to meet.

Reference materials were found in the following: *The 727 Scrapbook* by Len and Terry Morgan, *Airbus* by Bill Gunston, *Airliners No. 22, Fokker/VFW Fellowship* by G. Stieneke, *Airliners No. 25, Convair 880* by Jon Proctor, *Airliners No. 26, Convair 990* by Jon Proctor, *Airliners Production List* by Nigel Milton Tompkins, *Airlines of the United States Since 1914* by R.E.G. Davies, *Aviation Week and Space Technology* magazine, *The Big Eight* by Huber, *Bluebirds* by John Wegg, *Boeing—Planemaker to the World* by Bill Yenne, *Boeing 707 - Super Profile* by Christopher Chant, *The Captain's Log, World Airline Historical Society* by Paul Collins, *The Delta Family History* by George Walker Cearley, *Douglas DC8, A Pictorial History* by George Walker Cearley, *History of the World's Airlines* by R.E.G. Davies, *Illustrated Encyclopedia of Commercial Aircraft* by Bill Gunston, *Jane's All the World's Aircraft*, *Jet Airliner Production List* Roach & Eastwood, *JP Airline Fleets International* by Ulrich Klee, *McDonnell*

Douglas, A Tale of Two Giants by Bill Yenne, *McDonnell Douglas Aircraft Since 1920* by Rene Francillion, *Modern Civil Aircraft No. 5* by M. Hardy, *Modern Commercial Aircraft* by Green, Swanborough, Mowinski, *Observer's World of Aircraft* by William Green, *Societe Mun Ruc Ding Internacionale* by Don Keydicks and D. D. Mao, *United—The Mainliner Airway* by George Walker Cearley, and *World Aircraft Illustrated* by Champagne.

Visit your local library and find the entire world at your fingertips. The World Airline Historical Society may be contacted in care of Paul Collins, WAHS, 3381 Apple Tree Lane, Erlanger, KT 41018.

My own company, Airliners America/ATP, may be reached at 3014 Abelia Court #33, San Jose, CA 95121-2401, United States of America. Phone (408) 629-2121.

Introduction

Many books on this subject have been written. Many of them originated within Great Britain and thus were filled with more than their share of British-built aircraft. This book is being prepared in a chronological order by first-flight date. Aircraft will be shown by their primary type and then by their various dash numbers. Numerous photos were deleted at the last minute as space was limited. Perhaps the most unusual characteristic of this book is that the photos are from a working slide collection. You can actually buy copies of these 35mm color slides. Every photo in this book was reproduced from a slide in the Airliners America/ATP catalog, which is available from Motorbooks International by catalog number 111239.

Find a comfortable chair, sit back, and drift into a world of fond memories of our evolution into the jet age. Venture from days long ago when airport security meant a 4-foot-high chain-link fence where we were free to experience the smells of the ramp and the heat of jet blast, to the nineties, when security means loading bridges, sealed windows, armed guards, X-rays, and metal detectors.

Chapter 1

In the Beginning

From the earliest days of powered aircraft there had been one thing in common to all. That thing was a propeller. The propeller was a source of noise and vibration, it was expensive to manufacture and maintain, but, worst of all, a propeller limited aircraft speed.

Few good things come from war, but it was World War II that, for all its death and destruction, brought about the turbine engine. In the final months of that conflict both the Allies and the Axis powers had jet-powered aircraft flying under combat conditions. It was, therefore, only a matter of time until the jet turbine technology developed under war conditions would find its way into the civil airline fleets of the industrialized nations.

The early days were tough. In the United Kingdom, the DeHavilland Comet prototype first took to the skies on 27 July 1949. The first production Comet 1 flew 09 January 1951. Almost three years later, 02 May 1952, British Overseas Airways Corporation (BOAC) began scheduled service with G-ALYP, the first production Comet 1. From London to Johan-

On 21 February 1959, Douglas flew the first DC8-30 series airplane. Like the DC8-20 the DC8-30 had Pratt & Whitney JT4A engines. For longer range endurance, the DC8-30 had more fuel capacity. Pan Am ordered both the 707 and the DC8. Then, in what today could be prosecuted as ruthless competition, Pan Am informed both manufacturers that if they sold jets to Transocean, a California to Hawaii competitor, Pan Am would not buy any more of their airplanes. Transocean's Stratocruisers and Super Constellations were unable to compete with the newer jets, so Transocean folded.

In the United States, Panagra, Pan Am, and Northwest took delivery of the DC8-30 series direct from Douglas' assembly plant in Long Beach, California. Panair do Brasil, Swissair, JAL, SAS, KLM, and TAI were among non-US carriers receiving new DC8-30s.

In 1966, Pan Am began selling their DC8 fleet, which by that time had been upgraded to DC8-33s. Delta and United were the primary buyers. Shown here is a Pan Am DC8-33 landing at Miami in a strong crosswind. *Bill Thompson*

Apologies are offered for the filth and dirt in the emulsion and the grain of the Aeromaritime/UAT Comet 1 slide. It is our only slide of a Comet 1 with the original rectangular windows. Note the four-wheel main-gear bogies. The original Comet prototypes had very large tires and wheels quite like those on farmtractors. The fuselage length was 93 feet, and wing span was 112 feet. Four Rolls-Royce Avon 502 turbojets rated at 6,500 pounds of thrust each powered the Comet to a cruising speed of 480 mph at 40,000 feet. *Bill Thompson*

nesburg, with stops at Rome, Beirut, Khartoum, Entebbe, and Livingstone, the time en route was almost 24 hours. It was an adventure for the wealthy and privileged classes and all seemed to be going well. Then, in 1954, two Comets disappeared while in flight. Investigation revealed that metal fatigue was the cause, a cause aggravated by the rectangular windows of the Comet 1 and repetitive cycles of pressurization and depressurization. All Comet 1s were withdrawn from service.

That same summer, Boeing entered the race with the 707 prototype, the 367-80. The Dash 80's first flight was from Renton Airport, Renton, Washington, on 15 July 1954. Four days later the Comet 3 flew. The Comet 3 was ordered by several US airlines but only one was built. Ultimately the Comet 3 was used for intensive testing and development of the Comet 4 series.

Next to fly on 27 May 1955 was the French SUD Caravelle prototype. The first production Caravelle 1, F-WHRA, flew on 18 May 1958. Re-registered F-BHRA, it was the first delivered to Air France on 03 April 1959. The Caravelle was very distinctive in appearance as it was the first jet transport to have tail-mounted engines. The Caravelle was also the first jet designed for the sole purpose of serving medium-size cities in the United States or major European city pairs.

Not to be outdone, the Soviet Union flew their first Tupolev Tu-104 twin-engine jet less than a month later. This type was actually the second jet transport to see passenger service. Flying with Aeroflot, the Tu-104 was used between Moscow and Omsk with service commencing on 15 September 1956. Little was known about Soviet passenger jet development as the cold war was into its darkest days. The arrival of a Tu-104 at London's Heathrow airport in place of the usual equipment on a scheduled flight caused quite a stir.

Back in America the Boeing 367-80 had been racking up a lot of hours in flight testing and demonstration tours. The first production Boeing 707-120 flew for the first time on 20 December 1957, followed by the Douglas DC8-10 on 30 May 1958. Now in rapid succession first flights came for the Douglas DC8-20 on 29 November 1958, the Boeing 707-320 on 11 January 1959, the Douglas DC8-30 on 21 February 1959, the Boeing 707-420 on 19 May 1959, the Boeing 707-220 on 19 October 1959, and the Boeing 720 on 23 November 1959. In the British Isles, the Comet 4 had flown on 27 April 1958. The Comet 4C took to the skies with a first flight in October 1959.

The Boeing 367-80, prototype of the 707, made its first flight on 15 July 1954. The Dash 80 visited Orchard Field, site of what we know as Chicago O'Hare Airport, in 1954. The photo shows it on that visit with the early Pratt & Whitney JT3P engines. Boeing test pilot Tex Johnston was in command. Tex Johnston thrilled the audience with humorous and interesting stories of his test pilot career, particularly those relating to the 367-80, as the keynote speaker at the Airliners International 1990 Convention in Seattle, Washington.

This aircraft was used extensively over the years. It flew with three different engines at one time, the JT3C1, JT3C6, and JT4A. The 367-80 was also used to test different types of high-lift devices, and an aft fuselage mounted JT8D for the 727 program. Retired in 1962, the 367-80 was donated to the Smithsonian Institution. It spent many years in the Arizona desert and is currently in the Seattle area for restoration. *Jerry Modrak*

The SUD-EST SE-210 Caravelle. The earliest Caravelles used the cockpit section from the DeHavilland Comet. Caravelles from series 1 through series 6 were powered by Rolls-Royce RA 29 Mk522 Avons producing 11,000 pounds of thrust each. The Caravelle's length was 103 feet, 4 inches, and its wing span was 112 feet, 6 inches. The Caravelle's aft fuselage mounting of engines was quite unusual, perhaps even shocking, when it first flew in May 1955. Amazingly the prototype was flying before there were any airline orders.

The test airplanes had droop leading edges on the wings but testing showed these were of little value, and they were deleted from production aircraft. The Caravelles 1 through 3 had no thrust reversers but instead had a drag parachute in the tail cone. The Air France Caravelle shown, F-BHRA, still in service when this slide was shot in 1972 was the first production aircraft. *Eric Bernhard*

There were some attempts to enter the market that never quite made it. These are not shown in this publication simply because we have no color photos of the types. Even before the Comet a Vickers Viking was converted to the Nene Viking, so named for the two Rolls-Royce Nene turbojets. It flew on 06 April 1948. A Vickers Viscount prototype airplane, much smaller than the production models, also flew briefly with two turbojet engines.

In East Germany the strangest looking jetliner was made by VEB. It was called the BB152, with a capacity of 72 passengers. It looked like a Boeing B47 without the outboard engines. It had tandem landing gears under the fuselage and outriggers between the engines. First flight was 04 December 1958. The BB152

In North America, Douglas demonstrated a Caravelle powered by two CJ805 aft-fan engines, similar to those on the Convair 990. They planned with SUD to build the Caravelle under license at their Long Beach assembly plant. That plan was put aside when Douglas decided to build the DC9. TWA had planned to acquire twenty of these airplanes, one engine was even delivered to TWA's overhaul facility at Mid Continent International Airport north of Kansas City, Missouri, where it sat behind Building 2 for a year or so. TWA never took delivery of a Caravelle because Douglas had elected to build the DC9 by the time TWA would have been able to get funding.

United Air Lines ordered twenty Caravelle 6Rs. The 6R had a new cockpit windshield layout and thrust reversers. These planes served with United in the Eastern United States from 14 July 1961, well into the late 1960s. United operated two daily Caravelle 6R round trips between Chicago and New York. These flights were like flying men's clubs, allowing only male passengers. Think they could do that in 1993? The United Caravelle 6R shown overnight at Atlanta's Hartsfield International Airport on 11 November 1965. *Jon Proctor*

was destroyed in a crash not related to its design in 1959.

Within the Soviet Union the Tu-110, basically a Tu-104A with four engines in the root of a newly designed wing flew in 1957. There is almost no information available about the Tu-110. It was said that the four-engine transport operated VIP flights.

Little more successful was the Avro Canada 102. It had four each Rolls-Royce Derwent -5 engines low on the inboard of the wing. This plane flew mail from Canada into New York's Idlewild International. Howard Hughes wanted Avro Canada's

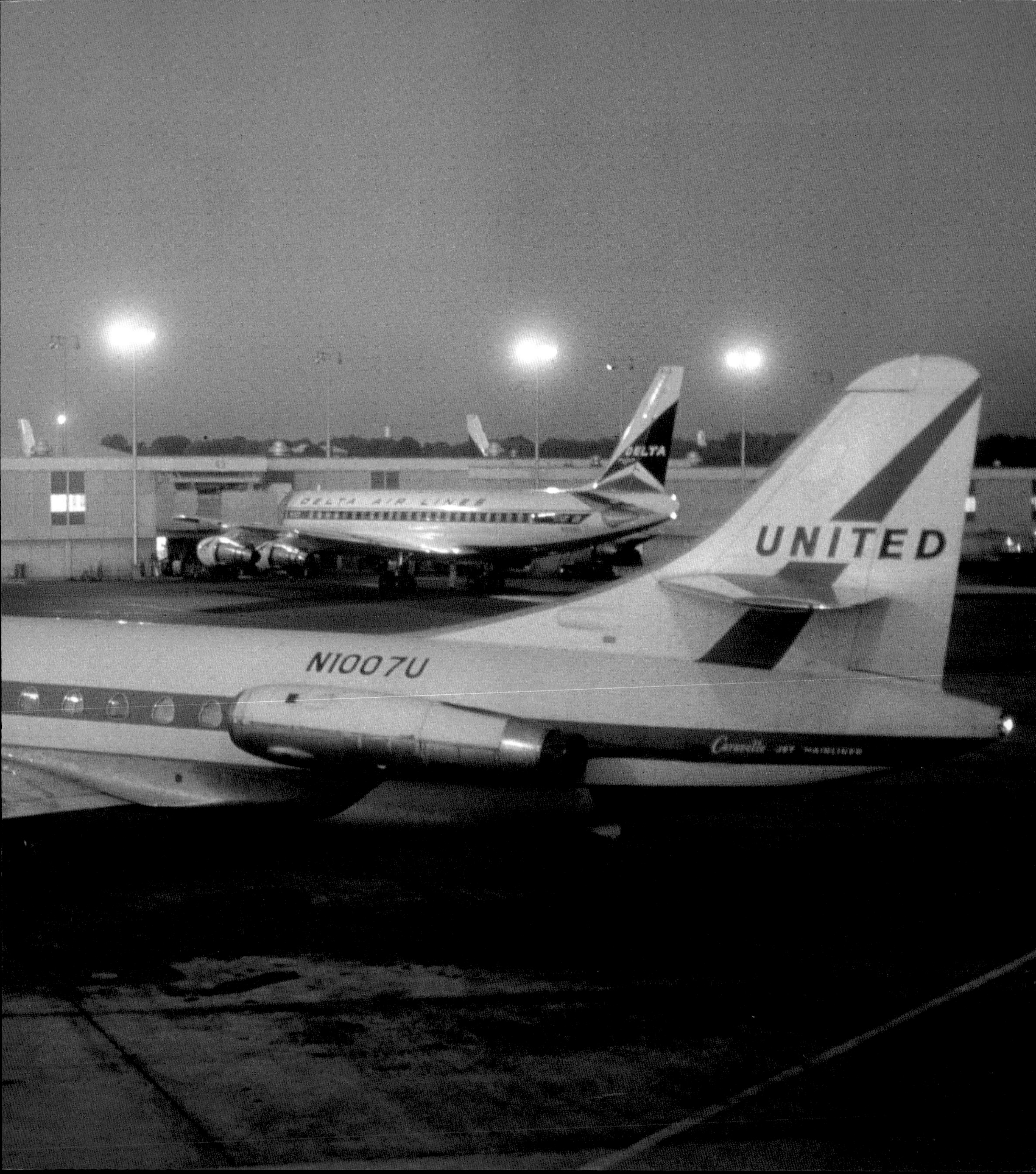
DELTA
DELTA AIR LINES
UNITED
N1007U

On 17 June 1955, the Soviet Union flew the Tupolev Tu-104, NATO Code Camel. It was developed from the Tu-16 Badger bomber. The Tu-104 was the second jet airliner to see scheduled service, with flights from Moscow to Omsk starting on 15 September 1956. Aeroflot and the Czechoslovakian airline CSA took new deliveries from the manufacturer.

The Tu-104's length was 126 feet, 4 inches, and its wing span was 113 feet, 4 inches. The Tu-104 was powered by two Mikulin RD-3M turbojets producing 11,000 pounds of thrust. The Tu-104B had a 3 foot fuselage stretch and entered service in the spring of 1959. This Tu-104 was photographed at London Heathrow in the summer of 1967. *Bill Thompson*

102 for TWA, but politics, available funds, and politics killed the project.

Now the world stood poised on the edge of the jet age. This book will show you what we flew in those early days, the bright metal airships that reduced transAtlantic flying times for that era even more than the Concorde did seventeen years later.

The Boeing 707-120, the basic domestic version, made its first flight on 20 December 1957. It was powered by Pratt & Whitney JT3C engines, the civil variant of the military J57, producing 13,500 pounds of thrust. Unlike the military version the JT3C had thrust reversers and noise suppressors.

Continental's 707-124 is shown at Chicago O'Hare in the spring of 1960. Note the short dorsal fin and absence of a ventral fin, an indication that full rudder hydraulic boost and dutch roll and yaw stability mods were yet to be done. The 707-120 was 144 feet, 6 inches long, max T/O weight 247,000 pounds. *Jerry Modrak*

You can tell just how attentive an airline enthusiast or employee has been by how they spell the name of the Australian flag carrier QANTAS. All across America you can find travel agencies that have spent hundreds of dollars to have airline names in gold on their agency windows. Chances are better than nine to one the name will have the letter "U" added. QANTAS is an acronym for Queensland and Northern Territorial Air Service.

Just as unusual and distinctive as that spelling is the 707-138. While we refer to the 707-320 series as the first intercontinental 707 this plane was intercontinental by virtue of what an automobile enthusiast might have called customizing. The fuselage was a full 10 feet shorter, which yielded a massive increase in range. QANTAS was the first non-US airline to offer 707 service. Note the short dorsal fin, no ventral fin. This 138 was on a layover in front of the old TWA hangar at the intersection of SFO's sierra taxiway and the ramp taxiway in August 1960. *Lawrence S. Smalley*

The DeHavilland Comet reappeared with the first flight of G-APDA, a Comet 4 for BOAC, on 27 April 1958. Trans-Atlantic service started between London Heathrow and New York Idlewild on 4 October 1958. The Comet 4 used four Rolls-Royce RAs. Its length was 111 feet, 6 inches; its wing span was 115 feet.

Note the longer fuselage, oval windows and wing slipper tanks of G-APDF in BOAC colors operating as Speedbird 937 from Tokyo's Haneda Airport to London's Heathrow Airport in the summer of 1959. *Mel Lawrence*

Douglas became Boeing's head-to-head competition with the DC8. The addition of wing slots and the familiar clamshell reversers at the back of a straight pylon of the DC8-10s made subsequent DC8s become DC8-11s. Further refinements to wing tips and wings yielded DC8-12s.

N8038U, a DC8-12, is seen here operating San Diego's first scheduled DC8 flight. *Jon Proctor*

First flight of the DC8-21 came on 29 November 1958. The biggest difference between a -11 and a -21 was the use of four Pratt & Whitney JT4A engines. Eastern operated the first passenger service with the -21 on 24 January 1960, IDL to Miami International Airport (MIA). Along with Eastern, National, United, and Aeronaves de Mexico (now Aeromexico) received new DC8-21s.

Eastern's DC8-21s initially bore the title "DC8B" but Delta petitioned the Civil Aeronautics Board (CAB), and Eastern was forced to delete that name even though at least one foreign carrier referred to their DC8-30s as DC8Cs. The titles shown in the photo stayed with Eastern's DC8-21s until the introduction of the newer 720 delivery paint scheme. The metallic gold trim so characteristic of Eastern's fleets from the late 1950s well into the mid-1960s was very expensive to maintain.

The Convair 880 first flight was on 27 January 1959. The 880 got its name from its 880 feet per second speed. In the United States TWA, Delta, Northeast, and Alaska ordered new 880s, Alaska's ordering being the only M version of that batch. The engines were single-spool General Electric CJ805s, a unique, fast accelerating turbojet also used on the Convair B-58 Hustler bomber. Most turbojets take about ten seconds to accelerate to takeoff power from idle, but the CJ805 would accelerate almost as quickly as you moved the throttle.

From my own experience I can say that it was a delight to taxi, very stable even at high speed on wet pavement. TWA pilots praised the 880's flight maneuverability. Among its other unique features, no outboard ailerons. Roll control was accomplished through inboard ailerons and flight spoilers. Built like a battleship, if you had to penetrate a line of thunderstorms and tornadoes this was the airplane in which to do it.

The things that killed the 880 were its noisy engines, heavy exhaust smoke, high operational costs, and overly complicated electrical systems. This photo shows TWA 880-22-1 in original TWA colors at Chicago O'Hare in the summer of 1961. *Jerry Modrak*

The Convair 880M was ordered by only one US domestic airline, Alaska. Swissair, SAS, Viasa, KLM, JAL, Cathay Pacific, and CAT all operated the 880M early on. Like the standard 880, the M version was a nightmarish collection of overly complicated systems. The 880M had retractable leading-edge lift augmentation in addition to extra fuel tanks not present in the standard 880. Some 880M aircraft even had lights in the cockpit to tell if the gear locking pins were installed.

While training JAL pilots and mechanics at LAX, a TWA mechanic asked the JAL people if they liked the 880. They replied affirmative. "Well good, we finally got even with you for Pearl Harbor," said the TWA mechanic.

Shown here is Japan Airlines 880M JA8025 Ayame at LAX for flight crew and maintenance personnel familiarization. *Jon Proctor*

*T*he Boeing 707-120, the basic domestic version, made its first flight on 20 December 1957. It was powered by Pratt & Whitney JT3C engines, the civil variant of the military J57, producing 13,500 pounds of thrust.

The Boeing 707-420 was ordered by BOAC, Air India, Lufthansa, Varig and EL AL. It was almost identical to the 707-320 except that it had four Rolls-Royce Conway Mk508 engines capable of producing 17,500 pounds thrust each. The Rolls-Royce Conway can easily be distinguished from the Pratt & Whitney JT4A by the oversized sound suppressor tubes and the absence of an oil cooler air scoop on the nose cowl. Conways had engine oil coolers inside the fan ducts. While the Conway was indeed a bypass engine, the small-diameter fan and resulting bypass ratio are why we did not place this version into Chapter 2.

Some carriers initially operated their 420s with the short dorsal fin and no ventral fin, but BOAC would not place the aircraft into passenger service until these stability mods were accomplished.

The photo shows an Air India 707-437 with the stability modifications in place at Tokyo Haneda Airport on 06 May 1961. *Mel Lawrence*

The 720 was Boeing's first attempt to capture the medium-size intercity markets. Almost externally identical to the 707-120, the 720 fuselage was 8 feet shorter. With that smaller cabin volume, two turbocompressors were sufficient. Most 720s were delivered with only two overwing exits instead of four, but Eastern ordered four exits, and some were later converted by other carriers for high density charters. There was extensive lightening of structures compared to the 707's structure; for example, the main gear wheels and tires were smaller than the nose gear wheels and tires.

The 720 had the extra leading edge Krueger flaps and the wing gloves that were used on the 707-120B and 720B.

The JT3C engine reached the zenith of its refinement in the 720. Most 720s were delivered with JT3C-7s, but Eastern 720s had JT3D-12s. There was no provision for water injection because with the newer hot sections it simply wasn't needed.

The photo shows Eastern's ship N8715E, a 720-025, at Chicago O'Hare in August 1962. *Jerry Modrak*

Aer Lingus, American, Braniff, Pacific Northern, and United also ordered the Boeing 720. The photo shows an American 720-023, N7531A, on a charter layover at St. Petersburg, Florida, on 05 September 1961. American later converted ship 531 to a 720-023B, modifying the engines to JT3D type. A lot of confusion was caused by American's use of the name 707 Jet Flagship and later 707 Astrojet after the conversion to 720B. Note the single overwing exit and no turbocompressor hood on number four engine. *Bernard Schult*

Improvements

After the first round of jet deliveries was over, manufacturers began deliveries of greatly improved, second-generation jets. The standard for engines powering the 707, 720 and DC8 became the Pratt & Whitney JT3D with thrust output ranging from 17,000 pounds to 18,500 pounds each. Lift augmentation devices, usually slats or Krueger flaps, used with the higher thrust engines, shortened required runway lengths and subjected airport communities to a little less noise. Aircraft were now able to climb to cruise altitudes much more quickly, so fuel burn was reduced overall. These refinements in themselves yielded a bit more range and allowed more revenue payload to be carried on long-duration flights such as Los Angeles to Tokyo, London to San Francisco, and even New York to West Coast cities.

At the same time, many new airframes were in development, the VC10, the Yak-40, the Tu-134, and the Il-62 tried their wings. Douglas went beyond the installation of Pratt & Whitney JT3Ds and stretched the DC8 airframe into three new versions.

The basic Boeing 707-120 when fitted with JT3D engines and full-span leading edge Krueger flaps and a glove inboard became a 707-120B. Consisting of metal ribs and fiberglass panels rising about 7 inches off the top wing surface, the glove was bolted right to the 707-120 wing. A new leading edge used with the glove from the fuselage to the edge of the inboard pylon changed the sweepback angle.

Shown in the photograph is TWA's N748TW, a 707-131B, landing at Columbus, Ohio, on 02 May 1980. This is a very significant airplane in US airline history. On 05 December 1965, this airplane was in a mid-air collision with an Eastern Air Lines Super Constellation. The TWA jet lost the number 1 engine, its pylon, and all of the wing outboard from that pylon. It landed safely, but, obviously, with a lot of anxious passengers and crew. Repairs were made and the airplane returned to service. 6748 from that time on flew with a new left outboard wing. *Ted Keener*

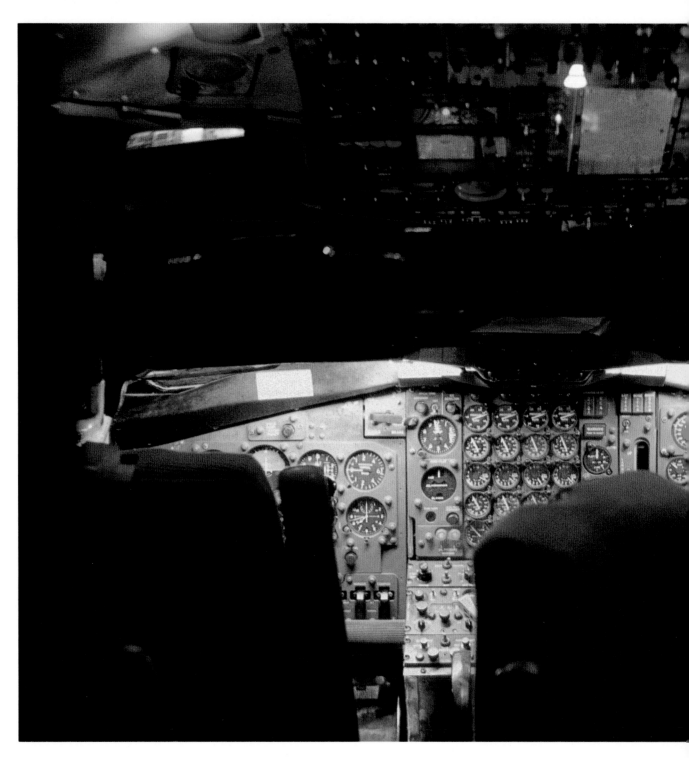

With the availability of the Pratt & Whitney JT8D engines Douglas introduced the DC9-10, -30 and -20, airplanes designed exclusively for short flight legs. Boeing took aim at the short- to medium-range markets with the 727-100, 100C and 200. With much shorter routes in mind Boeing also introduced the 737-100 and -200 to compete directly against the DC9. The JT8D also was used by SUD-EST to improve the Caravelle. Depending upon the airlines' specific requests the JT8Ds could produce from as little as 13,000 pounds of thrust to as high as 18,500 pounds of thrust. Early JT8Ds produced a lot of smoke with resulting heavy deposits of soot on tails and aft fuselage sections. A modification to the smokeless burner can in the early 1970s eliminated a lot of the smoke and yielded an unanticipated benefit: lower fuel consumption.

Within the United Kingdom, the DeHavilland Trident and British Aviation Corporation (BAC) One-Elevens were being produced. The Trident was to have been a bigger airplane than that which

The Boeing 720B, like the 720, weighed a lot less than the 707. Some carriers took great advantage of the 720B's lower fuel burn per mile to fly long, thin routes. Such was the case with Western. Some of Western's 720Bs were converted to what Western called the 720H.

Shown is Western's N93145 on the outer taxiway at the end of the TWA pier at SFO, 15 August 1977. By the time Western started changing their fleet to the bare metal "Bud Lite" scheme, the 720Bs were long gone. *Clinton H. Groves*

was ultimately produced but British European Airways wanted a smaller airplane. This delayed the first flight of the type to the same general time frame as the larger 727-100 and probably seriously hurt potential Trident sales.

Testing of the BAC One-Eleven had its tough times. One test airplane got into a deep stall and crashed. As a result of this incident and other incidents in flight testing, the appearance of the wing was changed significantly by the relocation and reshaping of stall fences. This may well have been the reason that today all T-tail aircraft certified in the United Kingdom are required to have stick pushers, devices that will lower the airplane nose thus decreasing the angle of attack.

Also within the British Isles, Vickers made the VC10 and the Super VC10. These long-range jet transports were designed to compete effectively against the Boeing 707-320B/C and the Douglas DC8-50.

The results of this development of new aircraft types and refinement of older jet transports fine-tuned the fleets of the industrialized nations' airlines. Many improvements were made in the late 1960s. Some used jet transports were finding their way into the hands of smaller carriers. Less industrialized nations such as Ethiopia, Columbia, and Argentina were now operating new jets. Airport security was virtually the same as it had been since the beginning, although closed concourses and jet loading bridges were becoming more commonplace.

Douglas continued refinements of the DC8 with the DC8-54/55 AF/CF versions. With a main-deck cargo door, strengthened cabin floors, and window holes plugged, the airplane was a dedicated freighter. When there were cabin windows installed, the airplane was probably convertible.

Shown is a convertible DC8-54 of Trans Caribbean Airlines at Boston's Logan International Airport. The extra hat-rack door on both sides of the cabin behind the wing would allow the transporting of passengers in the rear of the airplane and cargo in the front.

When Trans Caribbean was merged into American Airlines the latter sold the DC8s but retained Trans Carib's 727s. *Ralph Romer*

One of the earliest 707-320Bs is N762PA, a 707-321B. The San Francisco tower has just told the Clipper, "Position and hold Runway One right" one early summer morning in 1969. For photographers this used to be the greatest spot in all northern California. But terrorism reared its ugly head and a tall chain-link fence was built on the airport side of the creek.

Take a close look at the airplane. You can't see the sparse allotment of leading-edge Krueger flaps in this photo, but the ventral fin is very prominent. *Dean C. Slaybaugh*

There are exceptions to every rule. Case in point, the 707-351B in the photo. It has a main-deck cargo door installed at the time of manufacture by Boeing. The airplane was certified for operation as a "combi," meaning it carried a combination of freight and passengers. The "igloos" (prefabricated freight container) used were short on the port side so there was an aisle for the flight and cabin crews to use to get between the wheel house and the paying passengers. Northwest sold this airplane after a brief ownership. It flew frequently in and out of SFO with China Airlines of Taiwan in the early 1970s. Every trip she had cargo up front.

How can you tell it is not a C model? Take a close look. There is no "hat-rack door" aft of the wing. *Ralph Romer*

First flight of the Vickers VC10 model 1100, G-ARTA, was on 29 June 1962. There was only one model 1100, and in 1967 it was converted to type 1109 and was sold to Laker Airways, which in turn leased it to Middle East Airlines. The 1100's dimensions were 158 feet, 8 inches fuselage length and wing span of 146 feet, 2 inches. Its engines were four each Rolls-Royce Conway RCo turbofan engines producing 21,000 pounds of thrust at takeoff. The model 1100 had thrust reversers on all four powerplants.

BOAC's VC10 model 1101, G-ARVE, prepares to depart on a flight. Note the second cabin door ahead of the wing. This is the surest sign that this is a standard VC10. The Super VC10s have the second door of each side in an aft location right in front of the engines, similar to the aft galley doors on a 727-200. *Bill Thompson*

The Soviet Union needed a long-range transport. Ilyushin developed the Il-62, an airplane quite similar in appearance to the Super VC10. When the first Il-62 was ready for flight testing, the 23,159 pounds thrust each Kuz-netsov engines were not ready. The first flight, which took place in January 1963, was powered by four Lyulka engines.

One Aeroflot pilot who had defected to the west called the Il-62, NATO code name Classic, a death trap. Perhaps the new Russian government should pick a new presidential airplane.

The Cubana Il-62M CU-T1226 is shown landing. Note the thrust reverser doors are open even before touchdown. *Michael Mulligan*

On 05 December 1960, Boeing announced their plans to build the 727, a new concept in short- to medium-range airliners. Eastern and United both placed sizeable orders for the type. This was the first civil usage of the Pratt & Whitney JT8D, a powerplant that before this had been used to propel missiles.

A bold, pioneering design, the 727-100 had three tail-mounted engines. The center engine, mounted within the tail structure, was at the same level as the side-mounted engines, so an S duct was used to direct air to the center engine inlet. Each engine produced 14,000 pounds of thrust. As with most civil turbojet or fanjet engines, takeoff power is set by EPR, or engine pressure ratio. The S duct made a big enough difference that the EPR setting for takeoff at SFO was almost always 2.00 on the pods, 2.02 on the center.

For passengers the most noticeable difference was the absence of engine noise in the forward half of the passenger cabin. Up front engine noise on takeoff was even far less than the usual aircraft skin noise at cruise speeds.

Shown here is an Eastern 727-25 taking off from a Midwestern airport. Note the bright gold foil trim. *Bill Thompson*

In the late 1970s and through the 1980s, a fleet of three 727-100s was used for VIP transportation. First it was Regent Air, then McClain, and last MGM Grand Air. Passengers were treated to everything from limo service at both ends of the trip, usually LAX to JFK, an onboard secretary, a hair dresser, and posh seating. The example shown is a McClain Air 727-100 landing at LAX. We offer this photo to show one of the primary indications that a 727 is indeed a series 100 airplane. That indication is the galley door ahead of the wing on the right side. The other thing, except for Dee Howard Rolls-Royce Tay conversions, is the oval shaped center engine inlet. *David Campbell*

The DC9-14 shown here was originally delivered to Continental. In early 1968, Air California acquired two DC9-14s. These were in service until several 737-200s were delivered. Take a good look at the wing leading edge. The "potato chip" fairing is very obvious. The strake under the wing is called a vordilon.

This photo was taken at the old Slick Airways hangar at SFO in the spring of 1969. *John Stewart*

The DC9-10 flew on 25 February 1965. The number one airplane, N9DC, is seen being prepared for flight-testing earlier that month. Note that there is no "potato chip" fairing on the leading edge of the wing. The next photo of an Air California DC9-14 shows that fairing installed.

The engines used on the DC9-14 were JT8D-5s providing 12,250 pounds of thrust each. Later versions known as DC9-15s had the JT8D-1 engines rated at 14,000 pounds of thrust. There were no leading-edge slats, Krueger flaps, or slots.

Delta was the first airline to operate a revenue flight with a DC9. Two Delta DC9s had "DC9 Inaugural Service" painted on their noses. *Jon Proctor*

The Boeing 727-100C was designed by Boeing to be a quick change or "QC" aircraft. The external dimensions were identical to the 727-100 but there was a main deck cargo door added and the aft airstairs, unlike all others on the 727, would not lock into the down position.

A typical airline turnaround of this airplane would see it towed to the air-freight ramp where a large, sheltered vehicle affectionately called the Seat Eater would be driven up to the main cargo door. Airline workers would release the metal pallet sections, and the entire interior except for the hat racks and restrooms would be off-loaded in 30 minutes.

Great as the idea may have seemed at inception, the QC was an operational nightmare. Someone would always forget to take the evacuation slide off the galley door. It was supposed to remain with the seats. When the return airplane arrived around dawn, its cargo unloaded, the interior would be put back into place. Then it would be discovered that the galley door slide went with the airplane the night before. The result would be two cancelled passenger flights. As the seats and galleys were on pallets there was a heavy weight penalty, and, because the seats were 3 inches higher than in a plain 727, the top of the cabin windows would be at the passengers' chin level. Federal Express and UPS bought most of the 727-100Cs.

After a tragic midair collision with a military jet illegally doing stunt flying over the Los Angeles Basin, Hughes Airwest thought that perhaps the all-white fuselage of their DC9-30 may have been a contributing factor. The result, along with an official name change, was the "Top Banana in the West" paint scheme. The earliest paint jobs also added a silver mylar coating to the cabin windows but that proved too costly to maintain and the majority of the fleet had plain old clear cabin windows.

The example shown here, N9330, had been ordered by Bonanza. This wet February night in 1972 she sits at the gate across from the SFO employees' cafeteria in the old central terminal.
Clinton H. Groves

The McDonnell Douglas DC8-62 was the least stretched of the Super 60 series, just 6 feet, 8 inches longer than the DC8-50. Using a Pratt & Whitney JT3D-3B engine in a newly designed nacelle plus a new wing, the DC8-62 was the world's longest range airliner until the 747SP came along.

Here we see Braniff's DC8-62 bearing the work of artist Alexander Calder landing at Miami in 1973. *Nigel Chalcraft*

Perhaps one of those planes that's so ugly it just has to work right. The Yakovlev Yak-40 made its first flight on 21 October 1966. Its NATO code name is Codling. It was designed to operate from unimproved fields—grass, soil, or whatever.

The Yak-40 has three Ivchenko AI-25 turbofan engines, which develop 3,300 pounds of thrust each. The landing gear are retractable. Like the 737, the main gear wheels can be seen with the gear retracted.

The example shown, Cubana's CU-T1202, waits patiently for another load of passengers at Jose Marti Airport, Havana, Cuba. *Phil Glatt*

First flown on 09 April 1967, the Boeing 737-100 would be the 737 type produced in the smallest numbers. The engines were Pratt & Whitney JT8Ds of 14,000 pounds of thrust each. Only Lufthansa, Avianca and Malaysia-Singapore Airlines took new delivery of the 737-100 on their own. GATX Armco/Booth also had a couple that were short-term leased to several carriers including Aloha and Air California.

The fuselage length was 94 feet; wing span was 93 feet. Like those on the earliest 737-200s, the original engine nacelles were short. As a result, reverse thrust from the engines tended to lift the airplane off the runway. The long tail pipes shown on the America West example landing at Phoenix's Sky Harbor show the ultimate fix for the problem. *Greg Drawbaugh*

McDonnell Douglas continued to improve the DC8 series. Here is the DC8-63. It has the long fuselage of the dash 61 and the new wing and nacelles of the dash 62. Eastern purchased the DC8-63 because a CAB law judge had ordered that Eastern be awarded Pacific routes. President Lyndon Johnson—a Texan—overruled that order and gave the routes to Texas-based Braniff International and American. Eastern disposed of their stretched DC8s when it became obvious that they had been robbed in one of the most open cases of pork-barrel politics ever known. *Jon Proctor*

The BAC One-Eleven dash 500 was the United Kingdom's answer to the DC9-30. Seen here in the colors of Court Line, the dash 500 prototype flew on 30 June 1967. The wing span was 5 feet longer than the dash 400, and the fuselage was stretched to 107 feet, 4 inches.

Power was from two pod-mounted Rolls-Royce Speys. Most One-Eleven dash 500s are still in service, mostly with European charter airlines. *Dean C. Slaybaugh Collection*

Until the arrival of the 757-200, the medium-range airplane liked best by the airlines and customers alike was the 727-200. The dash 200 was powered by three Pratt & Whitney JT8D-7s producing 14,000 pounds of thrust each. Late-production airplanes had thrust reserves up to 17,500 pounds. With the galley gone from the middle of the airplane, the larger size of the cabin could really be appreciated. A typical flight for the 727-200 would be stage lengths such as Chicago to Los Angeles or St. Louis to San Francisco.

The wings of all 727s from the first to the last look identical. The fuselage was stretched 20 feet over the 727-100's fuselage, an even 10 feet fore and aft of the wing. The 727-200 is tail heavy, it is not unusual for airlines to require 15,000 pounds of fuel in the center tank for towing or maintenance taxi operations.

On the line this is pretty much a maintenance-free airplane. A typical log book squawk might be, "Please clean windshields." What to look for to tell this one from a 727-100? First, the center engine S duct inlet is circular, not oval as on the dash 100. Second, the galley doors are at the aft cabin just in front of the engines. The cargo-pit doors are larger and open outward.

Shown is N408BN in the colors of Pride Air landing at Miami, Florida, in 1984. *Pete Sampson*

The Boeing 737-200 was first flown on 08 August 1968, the early aircraft had short tail pipes. Such is the case with N462GB, one of six 737-293s ordered by Pacific Airlines but cancelled after Pacific's merger with Air West.

Air California's N462GB sat by the hangar ramp at SFO on 16 August 1969. *Lawrence S. Smalley*

Until 1989, one could take Lagoon Drive along the south end of Honolulu International Airport and rest under a huge Japanese globe willow. Now this area is a four-lane street and heavily secured employee parking lots.

The photo N730AL was shot from under that willow tree. The inter-island jets take off at an intersection well along the runway that goes deep into Hickam Air Force Base, so they are low and usually rolling into a 180 degree right turn to avoid rising terrain and the hotels of Waikiki. *Clinton H. Groves*

Back in Moscow, Ivan had been busy too. From the Tupolev Design Bureau came the Tu-134, a twin-jet transport with two aft-fuselage-mounted Soloviev D-30 turbofans rated at 14,990 pounds of thrust each. NATO calls the Tu-134 Crusty. The aircraft's wings have anhedral of 1 degree 30 minutes. VN-A124, a Tu-134A, is shown at Bangkok in the colors of Vietnam Airlines.

Next pages, this could be anywhere on the planet Earth—in this case it is Prague. A small accident happens and groups of people stand around scratching their heads and wondering, "What do we do now?"

How do they get the plane back on its nose? Usually one or two mechanics will enter the aircraft and walk forward. As they feel it begin to teeter, they carefully inch their way toward the cockpit. The aircraft will fall back onto its nose gear with no damage—maybe. *Jay Selman*

Chapter 3

Bigger and Faster

Prior to the introduction of widebody jets, aircraft fuselages had remained basically the same since the early days of piston airliners. The speed of sound, or Mach, was still a barrier, and when trying to add capacity to existing airliners, the answer had been to make the fuselages longer. Aircraft manufacturers in the United States in the early 1960s had believed that most all passenger air transportation in the 1970s would be by supersonic airliners. The original plans for the 747 were for a freighter able to handle side-by-side containers from nose to tail, thus the control cabin was above the main deck. Once it was realized that the SST would not become available, those plans were adapted to a passenger aircraft.

Now, in rapid succession, supersonic jets and twin-aisle, widebody airliners began to appear. At the same time, terrorism was beginning to cost the world its open airport observation decks. There was a whole new direction—airframes, engines, and electronic gadgets that had not even been dreamed about fifteen years earlier. The 747, "Fat Albert," the "aluminum overcast," had come at last. First flown from Boeing's new assembly plant at Paine Field, in Everett, Washington, on 09 February 1969, she was without com-

TWA's 747 service into SFO started very early in 1970. Ship 17104 was christened with champagne by Shirley Temple Black from a basket lift operated by fleet service foreman Steve Loe.

The 747-100 was 231 feet, 10 inches long, a dimension that is the same for the 747s through the dash 400 series. Wingspan was 195 feet, 8 inches. Maximum weight of the early aircraft was 705,000 pounds. With the addition of JT9D-7A engines the gross weight increased.

N93119, an airplane originally destined for Eastern, takes off in the scheme that was new in 1983. Note the engine-cowl sucker doors fully open and the tilt of the wing-mounted landing gear. The excellent low lighting in this photo shows off many of the intricate details of the 747. *Paul Minert*

parison, the largest civil aircraft ever. From nose to tail she was 231 feet, 4 inches. From tip to tip her wings measured 195 feet, 8 inches.

I shall never forget the first time I stepped into the cabin of a Boeing 747. That day at San Francisco International Airport (SFO) in the fall of 1969 I was TWA's maintenance coordinating foreman.

TWA didn't have a Fat Albert yet so I left the maintenance clerk in charge of the office and went with another foreman, Joe Amato, next door to Pan Am. There she was, Clipper *Young America*, N735PA. Her auxiliary power unit (APU) was running, and the sounds were quite unfamiliar. As the load on the APU would change, it would huff and puff. There were air-dri-

The Soviet Union, still involved with the Cold War, had a lot of international prestige resting upon their Tupolev Tu-144 Supersonic Transport. They were first—they beat the West. Their first Tu-144 flew on 30 December 1968. The Tu-144 flew mail from Moscow to Alma Ata and carried passengers briefly, from December 1977, to 01 June 1978. Serious vibration and engine fuel-control problems doomed this type.

CCCP-77102 is seen here landing at the Paris Air Show in 1973. She would never return to Mother Russia. On her next demonstration flight, the aircraft crashed in full view of the air show attendees, killing all on board. The probable cause was determined to be pilot error. It

was theorized that the pilot saw an oncoming press helicopter, thought it was much closer and on a collision course, and yanked the control yoke to the full nose-up position.

We don't know a lot about Soviet aircraft, but it is assumed that the Tu-144 had no artificial feel, or Mach feel, which most American, French or British jet transports have. These systems make the controls stiffer as speed increases. In a similar way, some automobiles have power steering that decreases its force as speed increases.

At least one other Tu-144 is thought to have crashed before the type was withdrawn from service.

ven hydraulic pumps (ADPs) at the rear of the pylons being turned on and off, emitting sounds like small rocket engines. As we climbed the mobile stairs at the R5 door and entered the E Zone (farthest aft) cabin, the enormity of the 747 struck us like something from a science fiction movie. It was sooo big! The smells of a new airplane are quite different from the smells of a new car. Through the cockpit and upper lounge, down the spiral staircase, and down the steps at the L1 (left front) door, we knew we were a part of history in the making.

Engines had their problems too in the early days. The JT9D-3 that powered the 747-100 had a tendency to overheat on starting. It took a lot of concentration to lower the condition lever to cut-off in time to keep from exceeding exhaust-gas-temperature (EGT) limits. Power was lower than promised. I flew TWA from John F. Kennedy International Airport (JFK), New York, to Los Angeles International Airport (LAX), California, in the first week of service. The engines were so weak we took 11,000 feet of runway to get airborne, and we didn't reach cruise at Flight Level 340 (34,000 feet) until we were south of Chicago. On reversing you had to put the engines into forward thrust before slowing to 80 knots or engines would ingest their own gasses and stall, sometimes sending flames across the top and bottom of the wings. Oh yes, when that happened you probably lost a handful of

Another major event of the early 1970s was the introduction of the Aerospatiale/BAC Concorde. One of the prototypes flew for the first time on 02 March 1969. This is a Mach 2 airplane powered by four Rolls-Royce Olympus engines with afterburners. The afterburners are used for takeoff and then for acceleration to Mach 2 after clearing land. Quite odd, the way the Concorde makes its ocean crossings. The aircraft flies like any other under air-traffic control guidance until acceleration to Mach 2. The Concorde will accelerate to Mach 2 and steadily climb to a peak altitude and then begin descending; there is usually no level Mach 2 cruise.

The British Airways Concorde was photographed from the ground at the 1986 Abbottsford Air Show. The only hint that this fly-by is not at altitude is the lowered visor. *Andy Abshier*

compressor blades and had an engine change to do.

Pan Am had the first scheduled revenue flight from JFK to London Heathrow (LHR), England. Clipper *Victor*, N736PA, flew the route after Clipper *Young America*, N735PA, was forced to cancel because

Air France also flies the Concorde. Here, F-BVFB is seen at Kerflavik, Iceland, just slightly southeast of Reykjavik, in the summer of 1977. *Ralph Moorhead*

of a mechanical problem. Pan Am mechanics quickly painted the name *Young America* on the left side of N736PA. Much later, N736PA was lost in a ground collision at Tenerife, the Canary Islands.

TWA had nineteen 747-131s on order. Of that order four were to have been East-ern 747-125s, but Eastern cancelled their orders, only to lease four from Pan Am. American Airlines ordered late, so they leased Pan Am 747s also. Among other US carriers using the 747 from its earliest days were National, Braniff, Northwest, United, and Delta.

Many people mistakenly believe that 747s with more than three windows on each side of the upper deck are 747-200s. Fact is, Continental and United had these windows added to their early 747s—at a cost of more than $1 million per airplane—so that theirs would seem newer to the average air traveler. As the 747-200 came close to production, some dash 200 improvements were included on late-production dash 100s. TWA's 17018 and 17019 had the new skins for extra windows, but TWA had them plugged for fleet commonality. Those last two TWA airplanes also had the −200 landing gear. Many people also believe that the only

powerplant used on a 747-100 was the Pratt & Whitney JT9D-3B and later the JT9D-7A, but in fact Saudia had eight 747-168Bs with the extra upper lounge windows and four Rolls-Royce RB211-524C2 engines and All Nippon received 747-SR81s with General Electric CF6 engines.

People worldwide loved the spaciousness of the 747. In the early days the traffic was too low to fill the airplane with paying passengers, so a lot of gimmicks

Singapore Airlines was the only carrier other than Air France and British Airways to have their paint scheme and titles actually appear on a Concorde. Braniff operated an interchange from Washington Dulles (IAD) to Dallas/Fort Worth (DFW) and even though an Airfix model kit shows full Braniff livery on its left side, no Concorde was ever painted in Braniff colors. The Singapore Airlines Concorde shown is at Washington's Dulles International Airport. *David L. Floyd*

Here we have a Trident 3, the final version of the type. First flown on 11 December 1969, a total of twenty-five were made for British European Airways, now part of British Airways. In August 1977 it was found that there existed a fairly serious problem with wing cracking. Wing panels designed to correct the problem were installed outboard. The new design had a resulting fuel burn penalty that probably hastened their retirement, which occurred on the last day of 1985. G-AZWB is shown here.

were used. TWA had a stand-up bar in B zone, American had an aluminum baby grand piano at the end of E zone. The first few years passengers had to fight the new technology multiplexing of electrical signals that allowed everything from reading lights and air vents to stereo channels to be controlled from their armrests. The early systems were a disaster. You would be reading on a night flight and your reading light would go out. You'd flip the switch and a reading light two rows in front of you would change. Worst of all, when the column timer decoders would begin to fail, reading lights, call bells, call lights, and air vents would chatter as if driven by an insane drill sergeant. Imagine eleven hours from SFO to Tokyo Hane-

The DC10-10 was the first three-engine widebody passenger aircraft. Locked in a head-to-head battle against Lockheed and their L1011, McDonnell Douglas' sales improved greatly as slow development of the RB211 engine delayed delivery of the L1011. The DC10-10 was referred to as the domestic version, even though Laker Airways used it in trans-Atlantic services. Powered by three General Electric CF6-6 turbofan engines rated at 40,000 pounds of thrust each, the type's first flight was from The McDonnell Douglas facilities in Long Beach, California, on 29 August 1970.

The number two engine was located in the tail, but, unlike the L1011's, there was no S duct. Instead, there was a straight air intake, with the dorsal fin and rudders located on top of the engine inlet. There were some DC10 incidents involving structural problems with the cargo compartment doors or uncontained engine failures. Despite those incidents, the DC10 earned worldwide acceptance by flight crews and passengers alike.

Shown is a Western DC10 at Fort Lauderdale, Florida, 01 August 1976, under a sky that says a lot about the fantastic south Florida climate. *Nigel Chalcraft*

Boeing's 747-100 had evolved into the 747-200. While the exterior dimensions were the same as for the 747-100 the -200 was rated at gross takeoff weights as high as 820,000 pounds. Now there were three major types of engines available. Many carriers went with the General Electric CF6-45, 50 or 80 varieties; some opted for the Rolls-Royce RB211-524D4, or JT9D-7R or 70 series.

Flight crews who have flown the 747-100 at max gross weight and then later the 747-200 have told me that the climb to cruise altitude abilities of the 747-200 are astounding. It was with the 747-200 that many airlines opted for a straight staircase with a landing instead of the spiral staircase. Some operators such as KLM had Boeing add the -300 series upper lounge with these airplanes becoming 747-200 SUD (stretched upper deck) and all 747s may have a main deck side cargo door in the E zone, this is known as SCD.

Shown taking off from Phoenix is America West's 747-200 N533AW, one of KLM's initial 747-206B series, powered by JT3D-7As. KLM sold its six Pratt & Whitney-powered 747-200s and converted their remaining General Electric-powered 747s to 747-206B (SUD) type.

da Airport (TYO) with the reading lights flashing in your eyes while you tried to sleep. The L1011 and the DC10 also shared the multiplex problems.

Airlines placing orders for 747-100s paid around $23 million per copy. TWA was paying about $2 million more for extra accessories. In 1993, the cheapest 747, a basic dash 400 series, sells for almost $160 million per plane. Most of each 747 is built of American-made parts. Boeing, without any doubt, is America's number one exporter.

In 1969 the Russians flew their supersonic transport (SST), the Tu-144; the French and the British as Aerospatiale and BAC gave us the Concorde; Douglas produced the DC10; Lockheed made the L1011; and Airbus Industrie flew the A300. Not since the Vickers Viscount or the SUD Caravelle had any European airliner been successful in America. Airbus Industrie, Toulouse, France, was producing A300s for which no orders had materialized. The socialist government kept pro-

ducing airframes in hopes that there would eventually be more buyers. Airbus approached Frank Borman of Eastern Air Lines with a proposition: four A300B4 Airbus types free of charge for a trial period. After all, what did they have to lose? The airplane was successful, and Eastern bought a lot of them. Quite a bit of the airplane was made in the United States—engines, landing gear, and much of the electronics—so there wasn't the stigma of buying a 100 percent foreign-built airliner. Soon, Airbus placed transports with Continental, American, and Pan American.

The Lockheed L1011 was delayed almost two years when the newly designed, three-spool Rolls-Royce RB211 engine had to be completely redesigned. Seems that the wide, lightweight "Hydrofil" fan blades were great—that is, until they did some testing in Saudi Arabia. It was found that sand would work away at the blades to the point that the engine could no longer produce takeoff power. Even when the engine was revised as the RB211-22B that powers all L1011-1, -50, and -100 series airplanes, avoiding overtemp on starting was a big deal. Unlike the CF6-1 on the DC10, the RB211-22B could take a lot of foreign object damage and keep right on flying. Dispatching RB211-powered aircraft with a few broken turbine blades is a common, approved practice.

Lockheed's L1011, unlike the DC10, relied upon one type engine. The Rolls-Royce RB211-22 initially had broad, lightweight composite fan blades made with a material called Hydrofil. When testing revealed that the blades could not tolerate desert conditions it was back to the drawing board. In the two years that were lost during development of a new engine Douglas made a lot of headway.

The L1011 flight control system was the first really new design since World War II. There was a stabilator-elevator combination without a jackscrew. The captain's and flight officer's control yokes could be operated separately through pulling the pitch disconnect and roll disconnect handles on the pedestal. Also, one up on the DC10, the L1011 had four hydraulic systems instead of three. System D was quite carefully placed out of the tail. When Eastern's N307EA bound for the Caribbean out of Newark had the center engine fan hub break, sending blades into the stabilizer and the pressure bulkhead, it was that fourth hydraulic system that got the people home safely.

The L1011's first flight from Palmdale was 16 November 1970. It was 177 feet, 8 inches long with a wing span of 155 feet, 4 inches. The Hawaiian L1011 came used from All Nippon. It is a -50 series, a -1 with slide rafts, HF radios and overwater navigation equipment. N765BE is seen at DFW. *Steve Tobey*

The DC10s had their share of problems too. The General Electric CF6-1 engine on the DC10-10 was very sensitive to foreign-object damage (FOD). One little AN960-8 steel cotter pin sucked up by that big vacuum cleaner could cause so much damage that you could look up the hot section tail pipe and see out the nose cowl. Two accidents involving the unwanted opening of lower deck cargo doors had people booking flights out of their way just to avoid the DC10.

Most of the time the Soviet-made Ilyushin Il-76, NATO code name Candid, is found doing military duties. The airplane is common among the Arab World with examples in Libya, Iraq, Syria, and other nations. The first flight of the prototype was on 25 March 1971. Powered by four Soloviev D-30KP turbofans, its length is 152 feet, 10.75 inches and its wing span 165 feet, 8 inches.

The Il-76 is perhaps the best transport the Soviet Union ever produced. It can operate from muddy fields, rock strewn terrain, and grass. It does what the C-141 and the C-5 should have done.

The Il-76 shown here is registered P-913, to North Korea's CAAK. *Martin Noack*

When Douglas built the DC10, they planned on three types, a domestic DC10-10 with General Electric CF6-6 engines, an international DC10-20 with Pratt & Whitney JT9Ds, and an international DC10-30 with General Electric CF6-50A. Japan Air Lines wanted a Pratt & Whitney-powered intercontinental DC10, but they balked at the DC10-20 designation, saying that this classification made it seem like less of an airplane than the dash 30, so, the designation was changed to DC10-40.

The first flight of a DC10-40 for Northwest Orient Airlines was on 28 February 1972. It was powered by four Pratt & Whitney JT9D-20 engines producing 49,400 pounds of thrust each. Shown is N149US at LAX on 20 November 1992. Note the trumpet-like flare at the front and back of the center engine inlet duct, just like the MD11. *Mike Rathke*

*H*ow do they get the plane back on its nose? Usually one or two mechanics will enter the aircraft and walk forward. As they feel it begin to teeter, they carefully inch their way toward the cockpit. The aircraft will fall back onto its nose gear with no damage—maybe.

Another airplane on its tail. This time it was Federal Express at the LAX freight terminal. Someone wasn't paying attention to the weight and balance as the airplane was being loaded. From the Imperial Highway side of the building the DC10-30F looked like it was trying to climb over the roof. *Michael Rathke*

Previous pages, SFO inaugural flight! This time it was Singapore Airlines on 04 April 1979. Singapore had been operating two cargo 707-338Cs in and out of SFO for a year when passenger service began. 9V-SDA was the first of around ten DC10-30s operated by Singapore until their A300B4s replaced them, the A300B4s were replaced much later by A310s. *Clinton H. Groves*

Beware of the new kid on the block! Airbus Industrie, a tightly bound group of European aircraft manufacturers, has begun to make the people at McDonnell Douglas, Lockheed, and Boeing quite nervous. Criticized for their creative financing, in one case even giving four A300s to a US carrier for a few months at no cost, Airbus seems to be gaining on their competition every day.

There were two Airbus A300B1s. One never saw service. The one that did is shown here, A300B1 OO-TEF of the European airline TEA. It saw a short-term lease period with Air Algerie. The first flight of an A300 prototype was 28 October 1972.

The A300B1 was 167 feet, 2 inches long with a wing span of 147 feet, 1 inch. It was powered by four General Electric CF6-50A.

The Airbus A300B2 flew less than a year after the A300B1 on 28 June 1973. Used by Air France, it had the same wing span and powerplant as the A300B1 but the overall length was 175 feet, 8 inches. When extra takeoff performance was needed Airbus came up with the B2K, K for the extra Krueger flap that filled the void between the slats and the fuselage. This was standard on the B4.

Shown is Eastern's N291EA at Atlanta's new midfield terminal. *David Floyd*

72

The DC9-50 series was a stretch of the fuselage to 133 feet, 7 inches, without an increase in wing span. The powerplants were Pratt & Whitney JT8D-17s. The DC9-50 first flew on 17 December 1974. Its first service was with Swissair.

In the United States, Eastern, North Central, and Hawaiian took new deliveries. Today Northwest has the largest fleet. This airplane does not like high and hot airports. Even taking off from Atlanta headed for Hartford, the added weight and smaller wing area meant very high takeoff and landing speeds. As a result, main wheel tire failures are a little more common on this airplane than on any other DC9 variant.

Shown here is a Hawaiian DC9-51 at the Honolulu International Airport Interisland Terminal in 1989. This is a great spot to shoot slides: just walk from the terminal parking lots north on Nimitz Highway and take a left at the end of the fence. *Jay Selman*

The Airbus A300B4 made it big on the world markets. So impressed were the Eastern management team that they placed an order for thirty-five B4s. They were registered N201EA through N235EA. Eastern also operated two former Iran Air A300B2Ks on the Boston to New York shuttle.

Airliners made in the United States are constructed with an aluminum alloy that has been coated with a thin coating of pure aluminum. This material is known as Alclad. It allows for fleet operations with bare metal. A300s were not constructed of Alclad. This is why we have seen no bare A300B1/2/4 series airplanes. Eastern tried to give the impression of bare metal by painting the A300B4 light grey.

Shown is Air Niugini's A300B4 The Bird of Paradise. They had leased this airplane from Trans Australian Airlines pending delivery of their own A310 which, regrettably, has a very plain and unimaginative paint scheme. *Martin Hornlimann*

Chapter 4

Refining the Art

In the early 1990s we are seeing a few new airframes developed. It is the established airplanes, however, that are undergoing improvement, a sort of fine-tuning of the types. The Russian Republics flew their Ilyushin Il-86 on 22 December 1986. It looked like an Airbus A300B4 with four Convair 880-type nacelles on steroids. Lockheed delivered their last L1011, this time a dash 500 model. McDonnell Douglas revised the DC9-50 into a Super 80 series, and as this book goes to press, the MD90 is in flight testing.

Camacorp came up with a CFM56 engine conversion for the Super Sixty series of DC8s, a conversion that added much-needed power and the benefits of a lower fuel burn and increased range. British Aerospace developed their BAe146 of which five different versions are flying.

Boeing's 757 and 767-200 flew months apart in 1981 and 1982; Airbus flew their

The 757-200 with Rolls-Royce RB211-535C engines entered service two years before the Pratt & Whitney-powered airplane. Eastern dominated the early delivery positions, and had firm orders for nineteen, with the option of buying twenty-four more. British Airways had a firm order for nineteen, with an option for eighteen more. The first flight of the 757-200 (there never was a 757-100) was on 19 February 1982. In the United States, engine types selected seemed equally split. Northwest and United opted for the Pratt & Whitney PW2037; Republic, American, and America West chose the Rolls-Royce 535E4 engine. Eastern's with the Rolls-Royce 535C engine were all upgraded to the 535E4 engine.

One of the questions I hear a lot is, "Why does the 757 stand so far off the ground?" Well, Boeing tried to stretch the 707 like Douglas had the DC8, but computer models showed that the tail would strike the ground before the airplane could pitch up enough to lift off, and landings could be even more difficult. The wings' angle of incidence could have been increased, but that would have created more problems, so they solved the problem by fitting taller landing gear.

The photograph shows a Boeing 757-225 with Rolls-Royce engines taking off from LAX during a sunny spell between passing showers in January 1993. *Jay Selman*

A310-200, Boeing came back again with their 737-300, 737-400 and 737-500 followed by their 747-300 and 400 and 757 parcel freighter. McDonnell Douglas came up with their MD87, MD88, MD90 and MD11.

Airbus Industrie was not standing idle either. In rapid succession they flew the A310-300, the A320-100, the A320-200 and after a few years the A340-300, A340-200, and the A330. Many of these airplanes are fly-by-wire types, meaning that

The Ilyushin Il-86, NATO code name Camber, is Russia's first venture into the widebody aircraft market. Capable of Category 3 (blind) landings, the Il-86 has four hydraulic systems driven by pumps on each engine.

The Il-86 has staircases built into the three lower-lobe cargo doors. For upper-level loading and emergency use there are eight cabin doors on the main deck. The wings have a 35 degree sweepback at the quarter chord. The center main gear carries four wheel and tire assemblies, and its truck seems to be the same as those on the main gear. The top of each wing has a shallow fence parallel to the line of flight and in line with the engine pylons.

The Il-86 interior is made from metals and natural materials to lessen the effects of a cabin fire. The Il-86 does have an Achilles' heel, its four Kuznetsov NK86 turbofans producing 26,600 pounds of thrust each. This thrust rating is about half that of Western engines, but the engine's fuel consumption is very high. As a result, a Moscow–Havana flight requires two en route fuel stops. An A310-300 or 767-200/300ER could fly the same route nonstop with a lot less fuel.

Shown here in the summer of 1992 at Moscow's Sheremetyevo Airport is an Il-86 bearing Transaero titles. The tail logo resembles both the Air France and Delta logos. *Charles T. Robbins*

The Aeroflot Il-86 in the photo is landing at Moscow's Sheremetyevo Airport in the summer of 1992. Note the similarities to the A300, including the windshield frames and the aft cabin windows sloping upward toward the tail. *Charles T. Robbins*

there is no direct cable linkage to the flight controls. Electrical signals are sent out from the cockpit crew through a "joystick," a handle looking like a computer-game input device. Maybe I'm too old-fashioned, but fly-by-wire scares me. On the other hand, the 747, DC10, and L1011 have no direct cable input to the flight controls. They have cables right up to the hydraulic control unit, but with no hydraulics there is no control. I guess that in another twenty years we will look back upon these new airplanes and see them as old, tired, and inefficient. Take a look at airplanes in their gates at any airport. Where there is a direct cable connection, the ailerons will always be opposite in angles of deflection. Outboard ailerons are locked out with the flaps up on older airliners, but on those with cables or wires to the hydraulic actuators you will see all four ailerons with their trailing edges down until there is pressure on the hydraulic systems. The Sioux City DC10 and Amsterdam 747 incidents show what can happen when all hydraulics are lost.

The Lockheed L1011-500 was designed for intercontinental flights. It had strange systems when compared to the L1011s before it. First flown in February 1978, The TriStar 500 used three Rolls-Royce RB211-524B4 engines.

The most unusual feature of this version was that the wing span was lengthened 4 feet, 6 inches without strengthening the wing structure. British Airways' L1011-500s were delivered without the extended wing; the wing extensions were incorporated later. To permit use of the extended wings, Lockheed used an active flight control system. In an upward wind gust, all four ailerons would deflect upward, thus damping some of the gust load. Just the opposite would happen when a downward gust was encountered. Also quite distinctive was the "Frisbee Fairing" under the center engine inlet. It reduced cabin noise and also lessened fuel burn. TWA applied these fairings to all their L1011-1/-50/-100 fleet.

Six Pan Am L1011-500s went to United when United purchased Pacific routes. United used them only a short time before selling them to Delta. Pan Am N513PA is shown here. *Tom Livesey*

The Super 70 Series of DC8 came about when Camacorp got FAA approval for an STC (supplemental type certificate) to replace the JT3D engines with SNECMA/CFM International CFM56-2 engines. These conversions were carried out in Tulsa, Oklahoma. Delta had Camacorp do one -71 conversion and accomplished the remainder of the conversions in their Atlanta overhaul base. First flight of a DC8-61 converted to a DC8-71 was 15 August 1981.

Converted DC8s had their type numbers advanced by 10. In other words, -61s became -71s, -62s became -72s, and so on. The -72s and -73s have strakes on the nose cowls similar to those on the DC10.

Here, a United DC8-71, N8070U, lands at San Diego. *Andy Abshier*

The Boeing 767-200 made its first flight from Boeing's Everett, Washington, facility on 26 September 1981. It was available with Pratt & Whitney JT9D-7R4D or General Electric CF6-80A2 engines. Many were converted to ER, for extended range, capability. TWA operated the first Trans-Atlantic services with the 767-231ER.

The FAA approved ETOPS (extended twin overwater passenger service) but many in the industry prefer to call it "engines turning or passengers swimming." I would not hesitate to ride a 767 from California to Hawaii, for in my years at TWA, I never saw one 767-231ER come into SFO with an inflight engine shutdown.

Shown here is N606TW, a 767-231ER. *Jon Proctor*

Right, compare the cockpit of the 767 to that shown in Chapter 2 and you will see why some people call the 757 or 767 "Pac Man." *Clinton H. Groves*

The 767-200 shown in American Airlines colors is a General Electric-powered 767-223ER. It is difficult for the untrained eye to tell the difference between the Pratt & Whitney and General Electric engine nacelles. Note the strange tilt of the landing gear bogies. Was this some sort or ingenious Boeing technology to improve landings? No such luck. I've been told the tilt is there because someone noticed too late that the landing gear would not fit into the gear wells. By mounting the strut at an angle and using a hydraulic actuator to tilt the bogie properly, Boeing was able to fit the gear into the well without having to do a major redesign of the airframe.

UPS ordered the 757-200PF (package freighter) from Boeing. The first 35 UPS 757-200PFs will be powered by the PW2040 engine. Later deliveries will have Rolls-Royce RB211-535E4 engines. The PF series has no windows. There is a single cockpit crew access door well ahead of where it would be on a passenger 757.

A UPS 757PF lands at San Jose, California, in the summer of 1990. *Clinton H. Groves*

Boeing stretched the 767-200 into the 767-300. The fuselage was stretched 10 feet, 1 inch ahead of the wing and 11 feet behind the wing. The 767-300 also has a retractable tail skid while the dash 200 has no tail skid at all. Engines could be Pratt & Whitney JT9D-7R4 or General Electric CF6-80As. The first flight of the 767-300 was on 30 January 1986. It was said that operators of the dash 200s could have them returned to Boeing for conversion to dash 300s. So far no carrier has opted for that.

Delta actually has both engines on their 767-300s. The domestic airplanes use the General Electric engines, and the international 767-300ERs use the Pratt & Whitney engines. Reliability is the reason, remember ETOPS?

Photo shows Delta N177DN. *Frank Hines*

Airbus wanted a longer range A300. They achieved this goal by shortening the A300 fuselage, redesigning the empennage, and replacing the wing with a supercritical wing. This modified airplane was dubbed the A310. The dash 300 version was also equipped with a tailplane trim fuel tank. Fuel in the tail helps keep a rearward center of gravity, a condition that increases fuel efficiency. Pan American used both the A310-200 and the A310-300. The aircraft shown is an A310-300. *Jay Selman*

The Airbus Industrie A320-100 was designed to compete against Boeing's 737-300 series airplanes. British Airways, Air France, and Lufthansa took early deliveries. The A320 is the only Airbus product where the absence or presence of the winglets determines the series. The A320-100s do not have winglets, whereas all A320-200 series do have winglets.

The A320 was the first commercial, subsonic aircraft to use full-time fly-by-wire flight controls. Joysticks that strongly resemble those in most video games are placed to the outboard side of each pilot.

This British Airways A320-100, registered G-BUSB, is shown landing at London Heathrow in the summer of 1991. *Jay Selman*

*M*aybe I'm too old fashioned, but fly-by-wire scares me.

Even more from Airbus Industrie, this time a longer range A300-600 called the A300-600R. The 600R uses a trim fuel tank inside the tailplane, just like the A310-300.

The American Airlines A300-600R shown landing at Miami International Airport is painted grey. American's 1992–1993 deliveries appear to have bare-metal surfaces, meaning that Airbus used Alclad for the skin, or that the aircraft were painted with a clear protective coating. *Jay Selman*

The Boeing 747-400 retained the same fuselage as the 747-300, but the 747-400 has an improved wing-root fairing, a 6 foot extension to each wing, and a 6 foot tall winglet on each wing tip.

There are some exceptions to the basic configuration. All Nippon and JAL are using some 747-400s as SR (short-range) versions. These do not have the winglets. Also confusing, the 747-400 freighter has the upper deck of the older 747-100. People will tend to mistake these two as 300 or 200 series aircraft.

While the engine selection is practically the same as for the 747-200 through 300, the nacelles are strikingly different in appearance. The Rolls-Royce nacelles are the same in appearance as those on later 757s. The General Electric and Pratt & Whitney nacelles are similar to each other, but not the same as on older versions.

Here is an example of the 747-400 using the Pratt & Whitney nacelles. At the end of a nonstop flight from Sydney, this incident at LAX in August 1990 damaged the nose gear doors of this United aircraft and rattled some nerves. *Brian Gore*

British Airways 747-400 G-BNLF approaches Seattle-Tacoma International Airport. *Greg Drawbaugh*

The Indian Airlines A320-200s are unlike any other. Besides having the IAE V2500 engines the Indian Airlines A320s have a four-wheel tandem bogie on each main landing gear. *Herman Trip*

The similarities between Western and Eastern aircraft are amazing. The VC10 is seen in the Il-62, the Concorde in the Tu-144, the Airbus in the Il-86/96. Now we present to you the "757ski," better known as the Tupolev Tu-204. Shown here is the earliest version at the 1989 Paris Air Show. *Charles T. Robbins*

Boeing's 737 was taken a step shorter in the form of the 737-500. Just 6 inches longer than a 737-200, the 737-500 uses the engines, wings and empennage of the 737-300. The first flight of the 737-500 was on 30 June 1989.

First deliveries were to Southwest Airlines; later deliveries were to United Air Lines. Outside the United States, Aer Lingus, Air France, China Southern, Czechoslovakian, Egyptair, Hapag Lloyd, LAM, LOT, Lufthansa, Maersk, Royal Air Maroc, Sabena, Sobelair, TAESA, and Turkish got early deliveries.

I had once asked a friend who has a high-profile job at Boeing, "Why would anyone buy the 737-500?" His answer was that it is several million cheaper to purchase than a 737-400 and the operational costs were lower too. The photo shows United's N902UA at LAX in October 1992. *Mike Rathke*

"Mr. Gorbachev, tear down this wall" asked Ronald Reagan in Berlin. Well, more than the wall came down, the trade and technology barriers fell too. So it is that the Tu-204 became even more like the 757-200 with the addition of two Rolls-Royce RB211-535s. That version is seen here landing at Farnborough in the summer of 1992. *Charles T. Robbins*

A irbus Industrie is going after the 747 and 777 market with their newly designed A340 series. Shown at Toulouse, France, is A340-300 F-WWAL.The A340s are all powered by four CFM56-5C2 engines of 31,200 pounds of thrust each. *Mike Rathke*

T he McDonnell Douglas MD11 is derived from the DC10 series airplanes. The type's first flight was from Long Beach on 10 January 1990. The MD11 is 200 feet, 10 inches long, and its wing span is 169 feet, 6 inches. As I prepare this text there should be three engine types approved for use on the MD11: the General Electric CF6-80C2D1F rated at 61,500 pounds of thrust, the Pratt & Whitney 4460 rated at 60,000 pounds of thrust, and the Rolls-Royce RB211-524L rated at from 65,000 to 70,000 pounds of thrust.

Like the DC10-40 the center engine inlet has a trumpet flare at both the front and back. There is a centerline two-wheel main gear strut between the main gears. Unlike its predecessors, the MD11 can carry trim fuel in the horizontal stabilizer.

Delta Air Lines ordered McDonnell Douglas MD11s. The one shown here is their own third airplane. I say "own" because Delta leased two MD11s intended for Air Europe for a couple of years. These lease airplanes have CF6 engines; Delta's own "keepers" have the Pratt & Whitney engine.

This MD11 was flown to Mojave, California, for further modifications. The winglets and engines have been removed. Note the location of the number 2 engine inlet. Many people seem to think the center engine is a lot longer but they are in fact identical with the minor exceptions of reverser cascade vanes, hydraulic pumps, and other bolt-on accessories. The same applies for the DC10, L1011 and 727. *Greg Drawbaugh*

Index